HowExpert Presents

K-Pop Survival Guide

A Rookie K-Pop Fan's Guide to Learning and Enjoying Korean Pop Music to the Fullest From A to Z

HowExpert with Hayley Marland

For more tips related to this topic, visit HowExpert.com/kpopsurvival.

Recommended Resources

- HowExpert.com – Quick 'How To' Guides on All Topics by Everyday Experts.
- HowExpert.com/books – HowExpert Books
- HowExpert.com/products – HowExpert Products
- HowExpert.com/courses – HowExpert Courses
- HowExpert.com/clothing – HowExpert Clothing
- HowExpert.com/membership – Learn All Topics from A to Z by Real Experts.
- HowExpert.com/affiliates – HowExpert Affiliate Program
- HowExpert.com/jobs – HowExpert Jobs
- HowExpert.com/writers – Write About Your #1 Passion/Knowledge/Expertise.
- YouTube.com/HowExpert – Subscribe to HowExpert YouTube.
- Instagram.com/HowExpert – Follow HowExpert on Instagram.
- Facebook.com/HowExpert – Follow HowExpert on Facebook.

Table of Contents

Chapter 1: What is K-Pop?

For those living outside of South Korea, you may have never heard of the term K-pop. K-pop is simply the name given to the South Korean music industry.

One of the most common and repetitive questions that K-pop fans around the world get asked frequently, is what is K-pop? For those living outside South Korea, you may have never heard of the term. However, K-pop is simply the name given to the South Korean music industry. The term K-pop is a combination of the words Korean and Pop. However, this doesn't mean that South Korean music is only pop music. Just like any other country, South Korea has a wide range of different genres and types of music. South Korea is known for producing not only catchy and addictive pop songs, but they are also known to produce beautiful ballads. In recent years, many K-pop artists release songs that incorporate electronic and dubstep sounds in their songs. Pop, dubstep, electronic and ballads are some of the most common genres in recent years.

Many people who randomly come across K-pop or happen to hear a song and don't know what it is, tend to wonder why K-pop fans that live outside of South Korea, listen to the music if they cannot speak or understand the language. Although there is no main reason as to why non-Korean speaking fans listen to K-pop, many fans have expressed that K-pop is like musical genres such as electronic or classical music. Although the listener may not fully understand the lyrics or the meaning of the song, there is still a beat and rhythm in which the listener can dance and hum in their head. There are also many K-pop fans that are attracted to the music, more specifically the music videos, as their music videos tend to tell a story unlike many American style music videos. K-pop is known for having bright and happy looking video clips, however, if you search a little harder, you will find bands that do concepts such as Cyborgs, Vampires, Witches, Time travel and more!

Many people also assume that K-pop is sung only in Korean as it is after all, Korea music. However, this is not the case. Within Korean music, it isn't uncommon to hear a secondary language, especially English. One of the best parts of K-pop is that many Korean artists tend to incorporate a secondary language such as English, Chinese, Japanese, Spanish etc, into their songs. Although many artists incorporate English words phrases into their songs, sometimes the translations and phrases can be a little questionable. It is considered uncommon for a song to be sung only in Korean. However, that is not to say that there aren't songs that are sung entirely in Korean. Many artists also release albums that are sung in an entirely different language. Many groups such as EXO or BTS have released full or mini albums that are sung entirely in a different language, most commonly Japanese or Chinese.

The Hallyu Wave

If you are a fan of K-pop, you may have come across the term Hallyu Wave. The Hallyu wave defines the mass spread and increase of popularity of Korean entertainment and Culture on a global scale. The Hallyu wave is also referred to as the Korean wave and is more commonly used in international media outlets. The Hallyu wave was notice in the 1990s when Korean culture and entertainment bloomed majorly in many countries across the world.

The Hallyu wave can also be referred to as the Korean wave, which is more commonly used by media outlets outside of South Korea. The Hallyu wave does not only refer to K-pop, it refers to Korean entertainment and culture. It is used when other countries and their people become fascinated of Korean food, culture, lifestyle and entertainment. Although the Hallyu Wave refers to the mass spread of Korean entertainment and culture, one of the most common and major influence of the Hallyu wave is Korean music aka K-pop.

It is only natural that K-pop is one of the most common and biggest influencers of the Korean wave. Although it is incredibly popular in Korea, over the past years, the number of international fans and listeners have been rapidly increasing. One of the main reasons is due to the rate in which technology is being developed. Due to the advancements in technology, the internet and technology is becoming more and more common for people of all ages. Technology can be and is accessed daily, making It incredibly easy to view videos and music from around the world. Because of this, international fans of K-pop can access Korean music and entertainment easily. Many international fans follow, listen and support their favourite Korean artists, simply by using technology and the internet. Video and music streaming websites and software's are also becoming incredibly popular by fans around the world. Thanks to the internet becoming easily accessible, the number of fans of K-pop is increasing daily. Many current and new fans of K-pop have discovered the Korean music and entertainment via the use of the internet!

Within South Korea, there are many different artists that have ridden or are riding the Hallyu wave. Many artists that have become successful in the international music scene, have since expanded their careers, not only in South Korea, but also other countries. Those who ride the Hallyu wave become well known, artists such as Psy, TVXQ and BTS are only a few. Groups that ride the Hallyu wave tend to have a large international following and presence within the music industry.

One of the most well-known breakthroughs within the Korean music industry, was accomplished by a male solo artist that goes by the stage name Psy. In 2012 Psy released the hit single, Gangnam Style. The song became an instant hit by people around the world. Fans became obsessed with the catchy beat and fun choreography. The song went on to be one of the biggest trends of 2012 and managed to become the number one song on multiple music charts across the world. Both the song and artist received worldwide recognition. The song was played on a wide range of radio and television programs and was viewed over three billion views on YouTube since its release in 2012. Since Gangnam Style was released, Psy has gained a large fanbase in both South Korea and in international countries, making him one of the most well-known K-pop artist to ride the Hallyu Wave.

Alongside Psy, there is an all-male idol group that has recently been achieving international success. BTS is an all-male idol group that consist with a total of seven members. The group debuted in 2013 under the label Big Hit Entertainment. The group has since been rising in fame and has recently captured the attention of international fans. The group is known for having a large international fanbase that spreads across the world. BTS is a well-known name within the K-pop community and is one of the most popular groups in the K-pop industry. In 2017, the group received attention from multiple international media outlets after they were nominated and received the Top Social Media Artist Award at the 2017 Billboard Music Awards. The group managed to beat well known celebrities such as Selena Gomez and Justin Bieber. BTS was also the first ever Korean artist to be nominated and receive an award at the Billboard Music Artist Awards.

Entertainment Agencies

To become an artist, you must become a trainee first and to be considered a trainee, you need to be signed under and entertainment agency. A contract is signed between the entertainment agency and the trainee. The contract holds the legal binding and agreements between the two parties. Every contract is different and is used to meet an agreement that caters for the demands and interests of both the trainee and the agency. Most contracts will have a condition in which the artist or trainee cannot legally promote or train under another agency unless approved by the agency signing the contract. As for how long a contract can last, that is determined by the entertainment industry and the trainee. A contract can last from a few months to a couple of years and are typically never cancelled unless both parties agree. However, there are some cases in which an artist may take their agency to court to legally cancel their contract. This could be cause by the agency neglecting or not fulfilling the agreements within the contract. An artist may also be required to pay a certain sum of money to cancel their contract. After the contract period is completed, the artist and entertainment agency may both agree to sign a new contract, however, it is also common for an artist to resign, but with a different agency. There are also many cases in which an artist has decided to form their own entertainment agencies and labels within South Korea. Instead or resigning or looking for a new agency, Korean artists and groups such as SHINWHA and Bi Rain, have formed their own agencies.

Within South Korea, there are many different types of entertainment agencies. Among them, there are three entertainment agencies that are commonly referred to as the Big 3. The Big 3 consists of YG Entertainment, SM Entertainment and JYP Entertainment. The Big 3 are well known within South Korea for producing and discovering talent in singing, dancing, acting and more. Artists that are signed under these labels, tend to gain recognition both before and after debuting, due to the popularity of the agencies. Many popular and well-known groups and artists such as Big Bang, EXO and Got7, are all artists signed under one of The Big 3.

Of course, there are also many other labels that are smaller and still well-known in the K-pop community.

Bighit Entertainment was once a small, not as known agency within South Korea until they debuted one of the most popular groups, BTS. Bighit Ent. was originally a small agency that was on the verge of closing its doors. However, due to the popularity of BTS, they are now a well-known name in the industry. Besides Bighit entertainment, there are also many other agencies such as Jellyfish, Cube and Starship Entertainment.

The purpose of an entertainment agency is to provide support and assistance to both artists and trainees during and before their career. The way in which an agency may support an artist, can be divided into two ways.

Firstly, an entertainment is supposed to support and assist an artist in their career. This means that the entertainment agency assists the artist by giving them the opportunity to produce, release and promote albums as well as providing them with frequent schedules such as appearances of television programs and variety shows. The agency is also meant to provide the necessities required to fulfil those schedules. This could include providing transportation to travel to and from schedules, meals, accommodation, staff such as managers and stylists; and more.

In most cases, entertainment agencies are also required to provide artists and trainees with a place to live and food to eat during their contract period. Some larger entertainment agencies give out meal tickets in which the trainee or artist can use in their cafeteria. Many artists and trainees are provided with a place to live which is typically shared with multiple other people. If an artist debuts as part of a group, the members will typically all live together under one roof.

The Life of an Idol

Becoming a celebrity is no easy feat for anyone. In most cases it is just a dream, however, within South Korea, there are thousands of people who are training to achieve their dreams. People who are working to become part of the Korean entertainment industry by going through strict and rigorous training are called trainees. However, even after completing your training, becoming successful and defining yourself as a well-known icon can be difficult to achieve. There are many different parts and stages that a person goes through before they can successfully debut within the entertainment industry and become an idol.

Becoming an idol singer or artist within South Korea can be an extremely difficult and long path that can easily take years of training and hard work to just debut! Before an artist can debut, they are put through training to prepare them will the skills and knowledge which they will require once they debut. Even if a trainee is given the opportunity to debut within the K-pop industry, there is no guarantee that the artist will succeed in the industry. There have been many cases in which an artist or group has debuted and then never managed to break through in the industry.

However, every artist starts from somewhere.

1. *Auditioning, Casting & Competitions*

Before even becoming a trainee, the talent of a potential artist needs to be discovered. There are many ways in which entertainment agencies find and recruit talented people to train and potentially debut under their agency. One of the most common ways of becoming a trainee is through auditions. Most entertainment agencies hold auditions several times throughout the year and over thousands of talented people from around the world to participate. Auditions are commonly advertised in several different ways such as through television or radio programs. However, there are also many agencies that advertise via the use of social media such as Facebook and Twitter, as well as through their own official websites. It is also common to see artists that are already signed under a label to advertise auditions. Another popular way to advertise auditions is by the sale of physical albums of artist that are already signed with an entertainment agency. Most agencies insert a paper leaflet with information regarding auditions inside of other artists albums.

Although the contents and process of an audition changes frequently depending on the agency in which they are auditioning for, many artists have told stories about their auditions. Many artists were required to sing, dance and show a personal talent. For those who manage to pass the audition, the applicant will typically sign a contract with the agency, as a result the applicant becomes an official trainee under that agency.

There are also many artists that have been discovered via street scouts that roam the streets of South Korea. Scouts are typically hired or are part of an entertainment agency and are tasked with searching and discovering new talent. Many artists have been discovered via street scouts for their looks and talents. It is common for people to be discovered when they busk or dance on the streets, which is a common occurrence within the major cities and entertainment districts in Korea. Popular idols such as SHINee's Minho and BTS's Jin, were both discovered by streets scouts. Both of which are now members of popular and successful idols groups within the K-pop community.

Competitions are also another popular way in which talent can be discovered. In America, there are many television programs that focus on finding new talent such as The Voice or American Idol. Just like America, South Korea also has television series dedicated to finding talent. Superstar K and K-pop Star are two of the most well-known and popular series within South Korea. The shows have discovered many artists and actors such as Akdong Musicians and Seo In Guk. There are also television programs such as The Unit or Produce 101 which are designed to not only discover new talent, but also give former artists or trainees the chance to be noticed once again, potentially giving them a second chance in the industry.

2. *The Training Process*

For an artist to debut with little or no training, is
extremely uncommon. Most artist go through
multiple years of strict and intensive training to
prepare them for the life of a celebrity. A trainee is
primarily trained in vocal skills as well as dancing.
Having strong vocals is important to any artist,
however, dancing is particularly important for artists
that are going to potentially debut as part of a group,
as being in sync is key to a good performance.

Many trainees are also given lessons in different skills
that they may require in the entertainment industry
such as acting, speaking, comedy skills etc. It's also
common for trainees to learn and participate in
classes where they learn an instrument. Some
trainees are required to go through classes in which
they learn how to speak Korean. It isn't uncommon
for trainees to be from other countries such as Japan
or China. In some cases, the trainee may only have
limited Korean speaking skills or no skills at all. Some
entertainment agencies may also make language
classes mandatory for all trainees.

There is no set time limit for the training period and
the training period can differ depending on the
agencies plans, as well as the skills of the trainee.
Training periods can last for many years, with many
artists having well over 2 or 3 years of training. Jihyo,
was a trainee for over 10 years before she was given
the opportunity to debut. In 2015 she debuted under
JYP entertainment as part of the all-girl group, Twice.
However, there are also many trainees who debut
quite fast. Hyuk from VIXX, debuted with just three

months of training after participating in a survival program MyDol.

3. _Debuting_

Once a trainee has successfully completed their agency is happy with the skills of the trainee, the agency will give the trainee the chance to debut into the entertainment industry. When the trainee debuts, they will either debut as a solo artist or as a part of a group or band. In most cases, the trainee and agency will determine whether they will debut as a solo artist or group, well before they debut. This is so that trainees who are debuting as part of a group, get to know the other members and so that they can all learn to work as a team.

Debuting signifies the start of their career as an artist. However, debuting does not ensure that the artist will find success in their career. The entertainment industry can be tough and unstable, to make it even worse, it is also an extremely competitive industry. Many artists that are given the opportunity to debut, remain unknown for many years. In some cases, the artist will simply fade out and leave the industry, but there are also times in which an artist is discovered later down the road. In 2017, many older groups and artists such as Nu'EST and WINNER, became increasingly popular. However, they aren't groups that have just debuted. WINNER debut back in 2014 and although they have been around for many years, they are only just starting to establish a strong career and gain popularity.

One of the major problems for those who debut as part of a group, is that although their group may have a strong presence in the K-pop community, it is harder for members to gain individual recognition in the industry. It isn't rare for a group to have a few members that are well known in the entertainment industry, however, there are members of groups who are simply known by their group name. For example, an all-boy idol group Madtown, has a total of 7 members and debuted in 2014. However, the only well-known member is Jota. Although the group has been around for so long, Jota is the only member that is well known, due to his active participation on variety show programs such as We Got Married or Cool Kidz on the Block.

4. *Building a Strong and Stable Career*

The entertainment industry can be fierce, especially in the K-pop community. Every year, hundreds of trainees are given the opportunity to debut. As a result, current K-pop artist need to be active for their career to survive. Staying active in the entertainment is the main way in which an artist can be noticed. Staying noticed and relevant in the industry is the main way in which an artist can build a strong and stable career. With so many new artists debuting frequently, it is important to stablish ones' self in the industry as soon as possible. The artists presence needs to be well known and have a strong impact to prevent their careers from fading away in just a couple of years. To make their career stronger, many artists turn to other forms of entertainment to become more well known in the entertainment industry.

There are several different aspects of the entertainment industry in which an artist can venture in to. It is common among artists to participate in musicals, especially if they have strong vocals. Since artists main career is music and singing, it is only natural that an artist may participate in the musical scene. Among popular artists, Jo Kwon is a popular musical actor. Jo kwon is a member of the all-boy group 2pm which debuted in 2008. The artist is known for taking on unusual and challenging roles such as a Drag Queen in the musical Priscilla. He has also gained mass attention for taking on roles in musicals such as On a Starry Night, Chess and more.

Another popular alternative in the entertainment industry is actin. Many artists pursue or establish an acting career alongside their musical career. There are multiple artists that are idols turned actors such as Lee Joon, a former member of MBLAQ and Ryu Hwayoung, a former member of T-Ara. There are also many artists that are currently still active in the K-pop scene who feature in films and dramas.

Staying active is important in the music industry and to do this, many solo and group artists, tend to appear on variety programs. As such, there are many artists that venture into variety programs and hosting. VIXX's N and Super Junior's, Leeteuk are well known for their hosting and variety skills and have both participated in many shows as either guests or hosts.

Chapter 2: What you Need to Know as a K-pop Fan!

Types of K-pop Groups and Artists

Compared to American Music, it is particularly hard to be recognized as an accomplished solo artist within South Korea. One of the major differences between American and Korean music, is that it is more common for music to be released by groups rather than individual artists. There is no doubt that America has produced well known groups, however, it is rare for groups to debut with over 6 members and for them all to be the same gender. It may just seem crazy to have a group with over 6 members in it, however, in South Korea it is a common and normal occurrence. Although there are still many well-known and established solo artists among the K-pop industry, Korean groups are more common and debut more frequently. In the K-pop community, there are various types of groups that can debut in the industry. This includes single gender groups (boy / girl groups), mixed gender groups and bands. Besides groups there are also solo artists and duets. Among these types of groups, it is most common for a single gender group to debut.

Solo Artists

Just like any other country, the South Korean music industry is also home to many well-known solo artists. Although groups are common place in the K-pop community, there are also many solo artists that debuted within the industry. A solo artist can either debuted under their own name or under a stage name within the industry. Within South Korea, there are three ways in which an artist can become a solo artist.

The easiest way to become a solo artist, is by simply debuting as a solo artist. This means that the artist is not part of a group and releases music under their own name or stage name. There are also many well-known solo artists that were former members of idol groups. A former group member may have left their group to become a solo artist for multiple reasons. This could be because the artist simply left the group voluntarily, by force or their group could have simply just disbanded, and they wish to continue pursuing their career in music. There are many former idol members that are well known around the world including HyunA or Jay Park.

It is also quite common for solo artists to still be part of an active and known group, all while pursuing a solo career. Artists tend to extend their music career by producing and releasing their own music that is separate from their group music. When an artist debuts as part of a group, all members are required to sing the same songs. This could mean that at times the music that the group is releasing and the music that a member wants to release could be completely different. By having a solo career, the artist can produce not only their own music, but also music as a group. Most solo artist that are still in groups, tend to release and promote their solo content when their group is inactive or are preparing for a comeback.

Within the K-pop community, there are many well-known solo artists that are still part of groups. SHINee's Lee Taemin, is well-known for his solo work as well as his work as a member of SHINee. He has released multiple hit songs and albums that were produced and released under his own name. As a solo artist, is has successfully participated in promoting himself as a solo artist via television programs, concerts, interviews, fan meetings and more.

Single Gender Groups

Figuring out what a single gender group isn't that hard. It is basically a group that consists solely of one gender. Single gender groups are the most common type of group in South Korea. Although there is both girl groups and boy groups. There is a noticeable difference in number of girl vs boy groups. Boy groups are more common than girl groups. It is also more common for a boy group to be in the spotlight. However, there are also many successful girl groups such as Twice, Red Velvet, 2NE1 and Girls Generation.

Being different genders, there are a few noticeable differences between the two, apart from their gender. Boy groups are commonly known for their powerful and amazing dance skills. Their performances are usually filled with a tight and difficult choreography that can be incredibly hard to learn. As for girl groups, they are commonly known for having either a cute and refreshing concept or a sexy concept. They too do dance, but in most cases (not all) their choreography will be not as tight and cuter, compared to boy groups.

Many people express their frustration between the double standards of girl groups and boy groups. Many people criticize girl group members regarding their appearance, stage outfit and plastic surgery procedures (which is common in South Korea even for non-celebrities). Boy group members also get a lot of backlash for saying certain regarding the opposite sex, as well as dating scandals and physical contact with the opposite sex. Many male idols have had their careers ruined by dating rumours, as well as scandals that never even happened! Even though the opposite gender may not be criticised as much, they still do get criticized in these areas, just not as often or severe as the opposite gender.

Mixed Gender Groups

Among all the types of groups, mixed gender groups are one of the rarest types of groups. A mixed gender group contains members that are both female and male. Just like single gender groups, they all produce and release music under one name.

Many agencies are known for attempting to keep their male and female trainees and artists separated, especially before or just after debuting. The reason for separating them by their sex is to simply reduce and avoid potential scandals and romance that could damage the artists career or the agencies name.

However, this doesn't mean that mixed gender groups are completely prohibited in the K-pop community.

Groups that debut as a mixed gender group tend to gain a lot of attention by the Korean media, as well as international and national fans of K-pop; both before and just after their debut. However, the attention fades relatively quick and many mixed gender groups tend to quickly fade in the K-pop community, leading to the group to disband or debut a second time, but as a single gender group under a different name.

Newer fans of K-pop may be aware of a group that just recently (2016) debuted as a mixed gender group that debuted under the name of K.A.R.D. The group consists of a total of 4 members, 2 of which are male and the other 2 are female. The group debuted under DSP Media and has been gaining in popularity since their debut, especially with international fans. K.A.R.D is the only mixed gender group that is currently active and well known in the K-pop community. As for older fans of K-pop, you may have heard of or was even a fan of a mixed gender group named Co-Ed School. The group debuted in 2012 with a total of 10 members. The group consisted of a total of 4 female members and 6 male members that later formed two sub-units that were divided by their gender, SPEED and Fve-Dolls. Fve-Dolls consisted of all the female members and SPEED consisted of all the male members. In 2013 their agency released a statement stating that Co-Ed school would no longer be promoting as a group, instead the group would be promoting in their sub-groups, SPEED and Fve-Dolls; thus, becoming two separate single gender groups.

There is no real reason as to why mixed gender groups do not thrive or succeed in the K-pop community. However, many fans have stated that they simply do not feel the same attraction or charms as single gender groups. Compared to single gender groups, mixed groups have too many inconsistencies related to vocals, dancing, costumes and skills due to the difference in gender.

Bands

To many people around the world, a band and a group may seem like the main thing. However, they couldn't be any more wrong. Although there are many similarities between the two, there are some clear differences between the two. In most cases a group performs strong and powerful dances to provide an eye-catching performance. However, a band plays all their music live. This means that instead of capturing the audience's attention with powerful dances, they deliver a strong performance by physically playing and performing their own songs with their own instruments. In most cases, a band will have little to no backing music when they perform, as everything is performed live. Most band members will have instruments that they play such as Keyboard and Guitar, however sometimes members can play many different types of instruments.

Although bands typically play their music live, there are some cases in which a band has danced or performed their songs in alternative ways.

Bands aren't as common as other types of groups and artists. However, there are many well-known bands within the K-pop community. This includes bands such as CNBlue and F.T.Island. Both of which are well known within the community and are the most successful bands. There are also many bands that have only recently captured the attention of the K-pop community. Bands such as Day6 and N.Flying have started to gain recognition for their beautiful songs and amazing skills by both international and Korean fans.

Fandoms

A fandom is a group of people or fans that follow and support the same thing. A fandom isn't strictly for K-pop. There are many different types of fandoms such as fandoms for television shows, music, books, games and more! However, in this case, we are referring to K-pop. In K-pop, fandoms are typically divided via the artist or group. Every artist or group will have their own fandom that support and follow that artist.

Fandom Names

Among K-pop fandoms, it is common for fandoms to be given official names. Official names are determined by either the entertainment agency or by the artist themselves and is commonly used by the artist to refer to their fans a whole. A fandom name is created to create a special and meaningful connecting between the artist are their fans. There are many different fandom names, however, some of the most fandom names that you may come across are ARMY, Starlight's, EXO-L, Monebebe, RedVeluv and Blinks. These are the names for the fans of BTS, VIXX, EXO, MonstaX, Red Velvet and Blackpink respectively.

Although it is common for artist to give their fans official names, there are still many bands that have not released an official name for their fans. This could be because the artist has just recently debuted. Many fan names are released on anniversaries that are important to the artist. This could include, their debut anniversary, 1-month anniversary, 100 days, or their first win. There is also some artist that are well known that do not have an official name. If an artist does not have an official name for their fandom, it isn't uncommon for the fans to create an unofficial name for themselves until an official name is released.

Fandom Colours

Just like fandom names, many bands have official colours that they promote with. Artist can have any number of fandom colours; however, it is quite common for a band to have just one or two colours. Fandom colours are typically used when an artist releases a new merchandise line or when they are promoting something via social media. Fandom colours are also frequently used by the fans themselves when they do fanart, write letters or when they design their social media pages such as twitter or Tumblr.

Fan Cafés

Within the world of K-pop, there are many different places in which you can connect with fellow fans of an artist as well as the artists themselves. A fan café is an official online website in which the entertainment, artists and fans can sign up to chat, follow schedules, talk about latest news that is all related to an artist.

Fan cafés are more common among groups and newer bands. However, due to the increasing popularity of social media websites and applications such as twitter and Instagram. Many artists and groups are trading fan cafés for social media accounts and pages. As such, there are also many groups and artists that do not own or run a fan café. So, if you live outside of South Korea and cannot read Korean. You are better off just following one of the bands social media pages.

One of the major problem about fan cafés is that in most cases the website will be entirely in Korean. It is extremely rare that a fan café offers an English version. Although there are some words that are translate into English, it is still hard to navigate and understand what you are looking at if you do not know how to read Korean. It is also difficult to initially sign up for a fan café without knowing your way around Korean social media applications such as Kakaotalk. Thankfully, there are unofficial tutorials in which fans who can read Korean create to show assist those who can't.

Fan Pages

There are several different types of fan pages among the K-pop community. However, they all have one thing in common, they are not officially related to the artist or entertainment. A fan page is a social media page which is run by a fan of an artist or group. Fan pages are commonly run on social media application such as twitter, Instagram, Facebook and in some cases Tumblr.

The first type of fan page is where a fan lives in Korea and follows an artist or group around on their schedules and take photos. This doesn't mean your simple quick snap of your camera on your smart phone. Many fan pages use professional and expensive cameras to take beautiful photos of artists during schedules and concerts. These types of fan pages typically upload their photos on their social media page. In some cases, the fan page may create some form of merchandise to be sold with the photos they have taken. This can be in the form of a calendar, photocards, photo book etc.

The second type of fan page is typically run by a fan that lives internationally or remotely. The page does not usually contain photos in which they have taken themselves. The purpose of this type of fan page is to mainly inform other fans of schedules and news about the artist, but to also share photos and videos of the artist. It's also a great place in which fans can come together to chat!

Following your Favourite Artist on Social Media!

In this day in age, it is considered unusual for someone to not have some form social media! Whether it is Facebook, Twitter, Instagram or YouTube, it is extremely uncommon for someone to not have at least one form of social media. As such, it isn't uncommon for an artist to have some type of social media account. Many artists use social media frequently, with many having multiple accounts on various platforms. Among the various types of social media, the most common among them us Facebook, Twitter, Instagram and YouTube.

Many artists will have two social media accounts on the same platform. The first account will be their personal account. A personal account is typically hidden from the public eye and is usually only shared with among friends and family. The second is their social account. This account is used to share moments with fans. Many artists post about their schedules, sneak peaks, news and sometimes just little messages to fans.

Social media isn't only used by the artists, it is also used by their entertainment agencies. Social media is used as a form of advertisement and is updated frequently with information related to the entertainment or artist. Most agencies will create an official social media page or account for each artist to share information and news.

Even with the increasing popularity and use of social media, there are also many artists that are either banned from social media or simply do not want it. Some artists believe it would be a major distraction in their already busy lives and that there is too much drama. However, there are also cases in which an entertainment may not allow their artists to set up or post on social media through personal accounts. Although it may seem unusual, it is common for entertainment agencies to restrict the use of not only social media, but also mobile phones among newly debuted artists and trainees.

Facebook

Facebook pages and accounts are typically run by the entertainment agencies, with the artists having limited or no access to the account. The page is typically used to inform fans of the release of new content, news, schedules and more. Facebook is basically the place in which an entertainment agency can freely promote and advertise an artist.

The entertainment agency themselves may also have their own separate page that is separated from the artist. The page can be used to promote all their artists in one place and only share major news. It is also a huge contributor in sharing information relating to auditions. Facebook is spread globally, as such many entertainment agencies post in multiple languages (Primarily Korean, English, Japanese and Chinese). This means that news can travel easier and faster around the world.

The easiest way to find an official Facebook page is by searching the name of the entertainment agency first. By doing so you will be offered suggested pages and in most cases the page will link their artists somewhere on the page.

Instagram

If you are looking for a more laid back and informal way to snoop into your favourite artists life, Instagram may be the way to go. Many artists will have an Instagram that is open to the public. The account is used to share many different photos and videos with their fans and followers. A majority of the time, the account will be run by the artist themselves and they will have full access to what they decide to share and post. This means fans can have access to many photos and videos of them doing things behind the scenes, selfies, photos of their travels, as well as glimpses into the artists persona lives.

Instagram also offers its users the opportunity to like and comment on the artists posts, as well as direct messaging. Although some artists have this feature turned off, there are many who still leave it open. Jessie who a well-known female rapper within South Korea, is known for her stunning selfies and sneak peaks on Instagram. However, she is also known for taking the time to read and react to fans comments and posts by liking and replying to comments.

Instagram also offers a live streaming feature which many artists make use of. Super Junior's Henry and

Kim Heechul are known for doing frequent live streams during their free time. Many artists live stream frequently to talk and update fans on a more personal level.

Twitter

Twitter is a combination of both Facebook and Instagram. In other words, it can be both official and more personal. Just like Instagram, many artists have their own personal Twitter accounts in which they use to share short updates with fans. However, it is also common for the artist to share official and important news with fans.

Entertainment agencies also commonly post on Twitter. However, due to the limited word count, many twitter accounts link off to a different social media platform or news sharing site.

Keeping Track of Comebacks

Comebacks are not only exciting for the artist, but it is also one of the most exciting and most anticipated time for fans around the world. It's a moment in which both fans and the artist has been waiting for! However, sometimes it can catch fans by surprise if they only just learn about a comeback a couple of days before, sometimes even after the comeback date!

Keeping up to date with your favourite artists comeback dates is important for any fan and it can sometimes be difficult if you follow multiple groups. However, there are a few ways in which can make it a little easier. Firstly, keep an eye on media outlets that focus on Korean entertainment and music. Two of the most common and popular names in the field are AllKpop and Soompi. Both websites follow and report on news related to Korean entertainment and music, it is also an extra bonus that both websites are completely in English. The websites frequently post about news and information on a large quantity of Korean artist, so it is extremely uncommon for them to not report on comebacks or debuts of artists and groups.

Another way to keep up to date is to follow all social media accounts related to the artist or group which you follow. This includes individual artist accounts, group accounts and account run by the entertainment agencies. In most cases, the artist and agency will post sneak peaks and previews, as well as promote their comeback on their social media accounts.

The final way isn't the best way to find information on comebacks but following fan pages and accounts can also be helpful. Although these accounts are not official, they are still run by fans, meaning they will probably post or share information related to the artist comeback. The only thing you need to check is whether the account is active or not. Simply check the date of the last couple of posts to see how frequently they update the page.

Chapter 3: How to Support Your Favourite Artists

Supporting your favorite artists and groups is one of the best things you can do as a fan. By supporting the artists, you are giving them the opportunity to grow and produce more music and content. There are many ways in which you can support an artist. Whether it is buying their latest albums and merchandise, or simply voting on awards shows. No matter who you are, how much money you have or where you live; there will always be an opportunity to support your favorite artists. Here are a few of the most common and popular way to support your favorites!

Buying Albums

If you have already bought an album, congratulations! You have already supported your favourite artist! Buying an album is probably the easiest and most common way in which fans can support their favourite artists. The best part about it is that you also get something in return, an amazing album! There are multiple ways in which you can purchase an album such as online retailers such as third-party websites or official stores, as well as by buying them in physical stores.

Buying Online

If you live outside of South Korea, chances are that the only way you can physically purchase an album is via online retailers. However, when buying from online stores, you need to make sure that they are selling official merchandise that will be directly and instantly counted towards music charts.

Many entertainment agencies offer fans around the world the opportunity to purchase albums and merchandise directly from the agency via official online stores. If you do happen to purchase via an official store, your purchase is automatically counted towards Korean music charts such as HANTEO and GAON.

However, if you happen to find a third-party website, it is extremely important to check a couple of things. Firstly, if the website legit? There are many people that purchase from websites that they have never heard of and get scammed. Make sure to do you research and see if anyone has written reviews or have previously purchased from them before. Secondly, check whether the merchandise is legitimate. In most cases, if you are purchasing from cheap websites such as amazon, eBay, wish etc, it is possible that the seller is selling copies of the albums! Make sure to ask plenty of questions and even ask for proof that they are real and official merchandise. Lastly, make sure that the purchase will be counted towards music charts. In most cases the site will advertise the fact that purchases count towards music charts, however, it is always important to check. Although you will still be supporting your idols as they will receive portion of the money from the sale, they will not be recognized on music charts.

Digital Albums

Buying albums can be extremely expensive, especially if you follow multiple groups or wish to purchase multiple albums. The cheaper option is to purchase songs and albums in digital copies. Most albums are songs are made available for digital purchase and download, with each purchase being instantly added to the chart. The best part about buying digital copies of albums, is that the digital albums tend to be cheaper in price since there is no production cost. Although you will still need to pay a small amount for the album or song, it can be a cheaper alternative. Although you won't have a physical copy of the album, it makes downloading the songs easier and you can put it on multiple devices.

Donating Via Makestar

The primary purpose of an entertainment agency is to support and path the path for their artists and their careers by providing them with the necessities and opportunities to do so. This includes providing them with events, comebacks, and opportunities to expand their careers. However, there is a countless number of entertainment agencies that cannot provide all their artists with these sorts of opportunities. Within South Korea, there are many entertainments that lack the funds in which are required to produce, manufacture and release merchandise and albums for their artists. There are also many artists that aren't legally signed under an entertainment agency and release and promote their work by themselves, which can be extremely expensive!

To give these artists an opportunity to promote themselves and their work, many smaller entertainment agencies turn to crowdfunding, more specifically, Makestar! Makestar is a South Korean, celebrity based crowdfunding website. Makestar can easily compared to other crowdfunding websites such as Go Fund Me and Kickstarter. The main difference is that Makestar is designed specifically for Korean artists and celebrities.

An entertainment agency may create a campaign for a specific project such as an album, music video or photo book for a specific artist. Fans of the artist can then make donations via the site and the profits will go directly towards the purpose of the campaign. Although the funds the fans give to the project are considered donations, many artists and entertainment agencies give back to the donors after the campaign has hit a milestone or when the campaign ends. The donors are usually given rewards based on the amount they donated, the higher the donation, the better the rewards. Depending on who is running the campaign and the artist, the rewards can vary from physical merchandise, skype calls, digital audio files or you could even get your name printed in the album as a donator!

Makestar isn't used by all entertainment agencies and artists, however, the ones that use it need help! As such, it's the perfect way to assist in helping your favourite artists grow and expand their careers!

Chapter 4: Common Questions about Attending K-Pop Concerts

What Should I Wear?

One of the most common, yet simplest questions that are asked by future concert goers, is what should they wear? Attending a K-pop concert can be extremely daunting when it comes to clothing and many people who have never attended a K-pop concert usually think that they must wear stylish and trendy clothing; After all, that's what they wear in K-Dramas... However, the answer is extremely simple, just wear whatever you want! The only thing you need to take into consideration is whether you will be comfortable. Most concerts last for at least an hour, maybe even two! Then you also need to take into consideration the amount of time you will spend lining up to go into the concert hall and you can't forget about standing in line for merchandise. You are going to want to make sure to wear some comfortable shoes, especially if you plan to line up early. Although you may look stylish and stand out, no one is going to be looking at you once the lights go dark and the artist starts performing!

You are more than welcome to wear whatever you want to a concert, however, it's always the better option to wear comfortable clothes and shoes such as sneakers and long pants. Of course, it isn't illegal to wear high heels and skirts, keep in mind that you will be standing or sitting for long periods of time without a break.

Many K-pop fans tend to wear shirts and fashion that match their idols styles. This could be done by wearing a similar outfit to the ones seen in music videos or an item of clothing that the idol has been seen wearing once before. Another fun alternative is to make your own t-shirts! It isn't uncommon for fans to make a shirt that has an inside or fandom joke on it, but you could also add things such as your Bias's name or the artists logo etc. There are many ways you can make your own shirts from paints to iron on transfer sheets.

Can I Record and Take Photos?

In most cases, you will not be allowed to record or take photos during the concert. Many Korean concerts forbid any use of recording concerts and frequently check bags of concert goers for any devices that could potentially record. Although phones are not forbidden from concerts, most concerts will have staff and security that monitor the crowd to stop people from recording. There have been cases in which people have recorded concerts and have been given warnings and removed for breaking the rules.

However, this doesn't mean that recording is forbidden at every K-pop concert. Whether or not the concert allows recording will depend on the artist, entertainment agency as well as the concert organiser. Even if you are told not to record, there are a few ways in which you can still do so during the concert... If you don't get caught that is.

Turn Down your Screen Brightness

Turning down the brightness of your screen before a concert is typically a good idea, even if you don't plan to record and take photos. Turning the brightness down doesn't affect the quality of photos and can reduce the chances of you being caught. In many concerts there will be security all over place, which is the same with any other concert. However, many K-pop concerts also have staff members at the concert that either sit/stand in the crowds or walk around the venue to stop people from taking photos and videos.

Turning down your brightness is also considerate to the other people attending the concert, especially those who are sitting next to or behind you.

Do NOT Zoom in!

Unless you have somehow magically snuck an amazing quality camera into the venue or you paid for front row tickets, it's safe to say that you are probably a fair distance away from the stage. This is especially true for more popular bands, however, the number one mistake many fans make when attempting to take a photo or video, is zooming in too far. Of course, you can zoom in a little without ruining he quality, just don't 100% zoom in. All you will be doing is ruining the quality of the photo and you may as well not taken a photo.

Don't Block Another Person's View

Recording or taking a picture at the concert is a great way to keep a memory and experience that will last forever, but don't ruin someone else's just for the sake of a photograph or video. At a concert you will be surrounded by hundreds and thousands of fans just like you. Fellow fans also forked out a lot of money to witness the performances, with some fans even travelling from different countries or states just to see them!

If you want to take a photo or video that's ok, just don't block someone else's view to do so. Don't stand up in the middle of the concert just to take a photo. There is nothing worse than paying a lot of money for a concert just to have your view blocked! Don't block walk ways or entrances and most definitely do not waste the time of others. Do what you must, just do it while being considerate of others!

Only Record a Few Things

Although you may think it's a great idea when you get there, remember this is a concert! It's supposed to be a live performance where you can sing, dance and scream your lungs out and nobody will judge you! If you were going to spend all the money so you could just look at a screen for a couple of hours, it would've just been better to invest into a better computer! There are many fans that would've like to be in position, so enjoy the moment! Being a K-Pop artist, you never know when they will return to perform at your city or country again! So, enjoy the moment so you won't regret! There are many fans who have regretted their decisions to film as they missed a lot of the concert because they were too focused on recording.

Not only that, there are also many artists that don't like it when fans record their concerts. It's not that they want to forbid fans from recording, so the event is private, but it's so that they can interact with their fans, instead of their screens. Don't get me wrong, there are also many artists that enjoy being recorded.

If you are recording, record a few things. Take a couple of good snaps and then put your phone down and enjoy. Although you may only record a few things, there will be many other photos and videos, whether they were taken officially or by a fan available!

How much will the Ticket Cost & Where do I Buy Them?

Buying Tickets

Buying a ticket to any event is already difficult, let alone buying a ticket to a K-pop concert! Ticketing for K-Pop concerts is one of the most stressful and nerve wracking moments for many K-pop concerts around the world. Buying tickets to a K-Pop concert or fan meeting is a race against time and it is extremely common for popular and well-known artists and groups such as BTS, EXO and Red Velvet to sell out in a matter of seconds! The fastest ever recorded sell out time for a K-pop concert was by an all-male group that goes by the name of EXO. In 2017, EXO's concert EXO Plant #4 – The EℓyXiOn sold out in a just 0.2 seconds. The record was set and is one of the fastest ever records for a concert to completely sell out of all tickets! K-Pop fans are crazy and fast when it comes to ticketing for events and concerts, even when they are outside of South Korea. Thus, if you have never done ticketing before, chances are you may not have a clue what you are doing.

When buying tickets, the official organizers as well as the entertainment agency associated that the artist is signed with, will release official information in the forms of news articles, posters and social media posts; with information regarding the times, dates, and prices of tickets. So, if you want to make sure you are up to date with information regarding ticketing, it's suggested that you follow the artist, organizer and entertainment agency before the concert! Once tickets go on sale, it is a rapid dash. As such, there are a few things you are going to want to know and do, during and before ticketing!

Ticket Types, Benefits & Pricing

K-pop concerts are just like any other concert or event! Tickets are commonly priced according to the position of the seats, as well as any additional benefits that may be included with the ticket. There are many different types of tickets that can be purchased. The names of the tickets typically change depending on the event, however they can typically be categorized in three main groups; standing, seating and mosh pits. The most expensive tickets are usually the mosh pits and standing tickets as they are the closest to the stage. Seating is commonly at the back and furthest away, making them the cheaper option. Depending on the organizers and artists, there may be addition benefits attached to the more expensive tickets.

Tickets that are considered Gold tickets or V.I.P Tickets, are typically come with additional benefits and privileges. These types of tickets are commonly the most expensive tickets for the concert. Although not every concert may include these benefits, many of them do. The benefits differ for each artist, however, Soundchecks, High Touch, Photo Opportunities or special merchandise packages are common among these benefits. Some concerts also offer additional benefits to lower paying tickets such as silver or bronze tickets. Although the privileges may not be as good as the higher paying tickets, many concerts hold raffles for the lower priced tickets which the chance of winning an opportunity to be included in the gold privileges or to win signed merchandise.

Note: Not all tickets or concerts may provide such privileges.

There is no set price of concert tickets, so make sure you save! Ticket prices can vary in price and the price will depend on multiple criteria. Tickets are typically priced based off the area, distance from the stage, the artist, organisers, venue, as well as the benefits or privileges that come alongside the ticket. Prices of tickets can vary from under $100 to over $500 per ticket! You will find that the tickets that come with more benefits and are closer to the stage, will be the most expensive ticket!

Another aspect that affects the cost of a ticket is who you are going to see. In most cases, tickets for solo artists will be cheaper and more affordable, than going to see a group or band such as BTS or Girls Generation. Why? It is simply that there are more members than a solo artist. The profits from the concert need to be split between many people. Not only do they have to pay for flights, meals, the venue, staff etc. They also need to pay the artist themselves. Meaning that the more artist there are, the more expensive the tickets can be.

Note: This isn't the case of all concerts.

Is it better to go in a group or by myself?

Attending a K-pop event can be both an exciting and daunting experience for first timers! No matter what sort of event you attend, whether it is a concert, fan meeting, gathering etc; it is perfectly fine to attend the events alone! One of the best parts of being a K-pop fan, is that the fandoms are usually welcoming to those who support the same artist, so making friends is a breeze. What is even better, is that It's quite normal for K-pop fans to attend events by themselves, especially outside of Asia. There are many people who go to an event alone and leave with a group of friends. As K-Pop is still growing in popularity, it is sometimes hard to find people with similar interests. And even if someone is a fan of K-Pop in general, they may not support or follow the same artists and groups. As such, events for specific groups such as fan meetings and concerts, are the perfect way to make friends!

Although there is no problem with attending events alone, you need to remain aware of your surroundings and safety. At most events there will be a lot of security (After all, you are going to see an idol!). However, there isn't security around all the time and you may enter places where you are alone, such as the bathroom. Although you should be safe, there is still the concern of stranger danger. If you do attend the event alone, try to stay in well populated areas or near security. Avoid going places where no one else is and where there are small groups. This also applies to when going to and leaving the event, especially if you are taking public transport! You never know what will happen, so make sure you stay aware of your surroundings and always keep a phone close in case of an emergency!

If you do decide to attend an event alone, make sure you check the age regulations of the event! Some events only permit entry to those over a certain age. This is common for concerts and events where there may be the distribution of alcohol or the music may be deemed inappropriate for people under a certain age. This is more common for music and artists that perform rap or hip-hop music. There are also some events that are open to all ages but may require minors to have a guardian accompanying them during the duration of the event.

Will there be Merchandise?

Attending a K-Pop event is already amazing on its own, what makes it better, is merchandise! Merchandise varies on several factors including the event you are attending, the artist, venue, organizers and the entertainment agencies. Whether or not there is merchandise is typically decided depending on the organisers, country and entertainment agency. It is common for popular and larger groups to have some form of merchandise for sale during the period of the event, however, that does not mean that there will be merchandise at every event.

Here have been cases where there has been unofficial merchandise sold during a K-Pop event. This type of merch is usually provided by the organisers instead of the entertainment agencies. Unofficial merchandise is more common among smaller and newer groups. Official merchandise is most common and will be at most events that have merchandise available for purchase. Merchandise isn't available for all events.

Events that are part of a world tour are more likely to have official merchandise that is supplied by the entertainment agencies. If the event does have merchandise, the organisers and entertainment agency will release information regarding the prices, line up time, and what is available before the day of the event. The information is commonly posted on the social media pages of the organisers and artists. Information is typically released a few days before the first concert in a certain country. There have also been some events that have not released information until just a couple of hours before the event starts.

As to what merchandise is available, typically depends on the artist and the tour. Some artists will have merchandise that is only available during the duration of the concert. There is also merchandise that is only sold in specific countries such as a greeting card or special card for the attendees of the concert. One thing you need to be aware of, is that merchandise can be extremely pricey! That's not to say that it is all expensive, but if you are planning to buy one of everything, you better start saving! If you are planning to buy a lot, it's recommended that you save at least $150! For older K-Pop fans, you may already understand the extremely high prices of K-Pop merchandise. But if you are new, here is a little information that may give you a better understanding. A standard official T-Shirt has can average to around $50 - $60 each and that is just a shirt! There are also many different types of merchandise such as clothing, light sticks, banners, fans, photo cards, photo books, albums and more! Be aware though, some concerts limit the amount of merchandise you can buy. Although it differs depending on the event, it is common for merchandise sales to be limited to 2 or 3 of each item per person.

Chapter 5: How to Keep up with the K-pop Community

K-Pop is one of those things that constantly change. There is always news on latest comebacks, scandals, rumours, activities, schedules etc. To stay in the loop about the latest news can be extremely difficult, let alone the news of an individual artist. Thankfully, due to the increasingly popularity of K-Pop and social media, it is hard to miss the latest trends. Unless you live completely under a rock or do not have a social media account, it is extremely hard to miss all news about an artist!

There are many ways that you can keep up to date with K-pop trends and the community. Whether it is on online fan base forums or live streams, there will always be a way to stay up to date.

Live Streams

Wanting to know what a celebrity is up to or what their private lives are like is a common curiosity that many fans across the globe experience. Undoubtedly if you have ever experienced this curiosity, you have probably already watched all the videos on YouTube you can as well as stalked the artists social media pages. However, did you know that many K-Pop artists do live streams? Live streaming in the K-Pop community is considered the norm, with many different artists and celebrities making use of platforms such as Instagram or Vlive that offer a live streaming service. For an artist, especially the newer generation of idols, to not live stream is considered unusual. Live streaming is commonly used by artists to share sneak peaks of upcoming content, as well as show fans glimpses into their everyday lives. It is also common for artists to do private live streams with the purpose of interacting directly with their fans by answering questions and telling stories! There are many different types of platforms in which idols frequently. And. although live streaming can be done on many different applications and sites, K-pop idols tend to stick to ether Instagram and Vlive.

Instagram is a well-known mobile application which is used to share videos and photos. The platform is used by millions of people around the world, including Korean celebrities and idols. It isn't unusual for Korean idols to have an Instagram account. The purpose differs depending on the idol, however, many share photos and videos of their travels, concerts, personal lives and behind the scenes content. There are also many well-known idols and celebrities that make use of Instagram's built in live streaming feature. Many idols such as Super Juniors Kim Heechul and Henry, as well as SHINee's Key, stream on a regular basis. The content of their streams varies but are commonly talking or eating streams.

The other popular platform for live streaming is Vlive. The application is available on both mobile and computer and is specifically built for the use of Korean celebrities. Users can create a personal account which can be used to communicate with the artists and fellow fans. Users also can follow specific artists and receive notifications when they go live. The primary difference between Vlive and other live streaming services, is that the application on always celebrities with an approved account to go live. Vlive also allows celebrities to upload official content such as variety shows, music videos and sneak peeks of content etc. Vlive is the preferred method of live streaming among many entertainment agencies and celebrities as it can be monitored in a more secure way. It is also used by newer generation artists that may have recently debuted to build a more solid relationship with their fans. There are currently hundreds of celebrities and idols using the application such as GOT7, VIXX, BTS and more. Vlive is also a place where idols stream typically under one account or a group account instead of individual or personal accounts.

Although these are just two applications that idols frequently use, there are many different applications that have been used in the past to livestream. Popular apps such as YouTube or AfreecaTV, have also been used in the past. If you are getting to know an artist, Vlive is probably the way to go as the application saves previous live streams, meaning that you can always watch them later!

YouTube

For international fans of K-pop, YouTube will be your new best friend! This is especially true for those who are living outside Asian countries such as Korea, China and Japan. YouTube is the world's largest video sharing and viewing platforms. Content can be uploaded by practically anyone, anywhere. As such, there is no better place to post new and exciting content. Many K-Pop artists rely on YouTube as a platform to reach the international fanbase. The site can be set in multiple languages and can be reached in places all around the world. By uploading the content, the videos can be exposed to millions of people around the globe instantly!

Many K-pop artists and entertainment agencies have official YouTube accounts and channels that are used to release music videos, news, sneak peaks, trailers and more! In most cases, the uploading and release of content will be monitored and uploaded via the entertainment agencies and will be used to release official content. However, there are also many celebrities that have persona accounts that they use to run their own channels in their free time. Although there isn't as many as other social media platforms such as twitter and Instagram, YouTube is the home to many individual accounts of celebrities. Artists such as F(x)'s Amber and Day6's Jay, are well known in the K-Pop community for the content that they post on their channels. Amber is known for releasing various types of videos that address problems, negativity and secrets of the Korean entertainment world. However, she is also known for her laid back and positive energy, which result in some fun and unusual videos ranging from watermelon splashing to cooking challenges!

There are also many K-Pop fans who make use of YouTube! Fans of K-Pop are also known for creating and sharing different types of content such as guide videos, compilations, reaction videos and more. YouTube is a great way to learn about your favourite artists personalities, traits, habits and lives. There are many fans that share videos and information that you may have never seen before! YouTube is definitely a great place for a newer fan of K-Pop or an artist to get to know the artist! So, if you are looking for something to fangirl too, YouTube is the perfect place to begin your search.

Social Media

Social media is they key in which many of us discover the latest news and trends. Just like anything else on the internet, the K-Pop is commonly being highly influenced by the content that is posted on social media platforms such as Twitter or Facebook. Many K-Pop artists and entertainment agencies have their own social media accounts. The content in which is shared varies depending on the artists, however, you are bound to discover fun facts or something interesting on these accounts. The artists also tend to post information on their latest activities or selfies. So, you will be kept in the loop of what your artists are up to!

Social Media is also accessed by the fans of K-Pop. Meaning you can meet and discover fellow fans that enjoy and support the same artists that you do! The best part about meeting fellow fans, is they are bound to know information about your artists that you may not have. They could also have information on their content, concerts and activities both internationally and in Korea.

Online Forums & Korean News Sites

There are many online websites that are designed for English speaking users. Popular sites among the English K-Pop community include sites such as Soompi, AllKpop and Koreaboo. These sites update on a frequent basis and release articles on rumors, news and updates on Korean celebrities. There are also many smaller K-Pop and Korean entertainment blogs and sites that can be easily found by searching on google or blogging platforms such as Tumblr or WordPress!

However, although these sites are news outlets, many fans have expressed their anger at these sites due to the increase of false or miscommunicated news and rumors. There are also times in which the outlets have accidently mistranslated or misunderstood the words in which a celebrity has said, which ends up causing a scandal or major drama in both the fanbase and celebrities lives. As such, you shouldn't believe every article you read! There are always going to be articles that make the situation look worse than it is or make it more interesting by throwing a few lies in the mix.

Another benefit of this site is that some of the sites offer their users the opportunity to not only make a private profile, but also give them the opportunity to post and comment on an online Korean entertainment-based forum. In most cases, the user will be required to create and verify their accounts to post and comment on the forums. Users can post and discuss a wide variety of topics such as latest news, scandals, comebacks, artists etc. Forums are not on every Korean entertainment website; however, a lot of these sites still offer a commenting system in which you can comment on the articles you are reading!

When reading information off these websites, it is always important to cross reference with other news outlets, as there may be additional information or information that may not match to other articles. Always make sure you do your research before you write a comment directed at another person. Although it isn't a set rule, always remember your netiquette when posting or replying to comments and topics. You are always going to come across people who have different opinions than yourself, so instead of full out abusing them, have a healthy debate and conversation with them! You may even make a friend or see something in a different. And admit it, both you are and the person you are speaking to will appreciate having an educational conversation rather then an abusive fight for the world to see!

Chapter 6: Starting your K-Pop Collection

Starting your K-Pop collection can be one of the most exciting moments for a K-Pop fan (after comebacks that is). Although it may seem like an easy thing to do. Many people don't know where to start or how to buy items. As K-Pop goods can be expensive, many people worry about getting scammed and whether the items they are buying are worth the price! However, if you know what you are doing it can be as simple as writing your name! There are many ways in which you can save money and buy more for less.

To help you start your collection, here are a few tips and tricks that you may want to know before you hit that check out button!

How to Buy More for Less

Today is the day, you go online to an official store. You put all the items that you've wanted for ages in a basket. You are about to buy your first ever album, everything is going great. Everything is in stock, you even managed to get a first-time spender discount. You fill in your private information and then you click checkout. You already knew the price of the merchandise, so you were prepared. You scroll down to confirm payment and then you see it. One of the biggest fears of a K-Pop collector, the shipping fees.

It may seem a bit over exaggerated, but many fans both old and new, have a heart attack when they see the cost of shipping. Getting an album shipped internationally can easily cost over double, even triple of the original price of the actual album. Due to shipping costs many fans don't even buy physical versions of albums and settle for just buying digital versions.

Buying online is the most common and frequent wat to buy K-Pop Merchandise, especially if you are just starting your collection. However, many new fans make the mistake of paying too much for the item and shipping. If you want to try and buy as many items that you can for the cheapest price, the following information, may just do the trick!

Tip 1: Wait for Sales

The easiest way to save money on K-Pop merchandise is to simply wait until the items you want to purchase are on sale. Many K-pop fans make the mistake of purchasing the albums straight away after it is released, however, it doesn't really matter when you purchase it, the funds will support the band. If you can be patient enough to wait, many online websites will have seasonal websites for holidays such as Christmas, new year's maybe even Halloween. Prices can easily be cut from 10% to 60% simply by a sale. If you are willing to wait, you could get more for less if there is some sort of promotion or sale on.

There are also some albums that are discounted as the store no longer wishes to sell or stock those items! The only time you should buy merchandise straight away is when the item is limited edition or signed as you may have difficulty buying it in the future, or the price may increase dramatically.

Tip 2: Buy multiple items at once

One of the major problems with K-Pop merchandise, is that you can easily pay over $60 for shipping! Since merchandise is from South Korea, you may also have to pay an importation tax depending on your countries laws. So, if you are going to spend that much money on shipping, you might as well go all out and buy more merchandise and albums. Most of the time, adding an additional item will not affect the shipping majorly unless it is extremely heavy. Most albums are usually around the weight; however, it usually depends on how thick the photobook as well as what content is inside.

Many online retailers offer their customers free or discounted shipping for first time shoppers! There are also many stores that offer events during holidays such as Christmas and Chuseok, which is a Korean harvest festival and holiday. Some websites may also have thresholds for free shipping e.g. spend $69 to qualify for free shipping. These websites will be your best friends, so make sure to check them out. These events can be a life saver for shipping fee sufferers.

Tip 3: Buy in Groups or with Friends & Family

The best way to reduce the cost of shipping, is by ordering with other people. Paying shipping fees by yourself can and will most likely will, be extremely pricey! If you are buying multiple items, then it may not bother you too much. But if you are buying only one or two items, there is no real point in paying such high shipping fees! If you want to make the shipping fees a little cheaper, your best option is to order you items alongside someone else's. Ordering with a group of people can help reduce the shipping fee, as the fee is split depending on the number of people and the number of items that each person ordered.

There are several ways in which you can order as a group. Firstly, you could either join or start your own group order for an item. Most group orders only order one item at a time, so if you are wanting to buy more than one type of item, you may prefer the second option! Option number two is to order with your friends and family. If you are buying on an online website, simply ask if anyone wants to order from the site you are using. This is also the safer option as you will know the people who will be ordering, and you can manage the purchase yourself!

Tip 4: Compare the Weight of Items!

You have probably figured out from the last few tips that shipping fee is what makes K-Pop merchandise so expensive! In fact, K-pop merchandise is reasonably priced most of the time. This tip may seem silly, but it is a smart way to save money. The main reason for high shipping fees is sometimes due to the weight of the merchandise in which you have purchased. As such, the lighter the item, the less it is going to cost to get shipped.

Most online retailers will list the weight of the item on either the picture or in the item description. If you are planning to buy a ton of items, try and divide them by weight. E.g., send all the heavy ones together and all the light ones together. This way, you will pay less shipping. Not many fans take into consideration the weight of the items that they purchase.

Looking at the weight of an item can also help you decide what you really want. If you have a list of items but they are extremely heavy. Do maths! See how many albums you can get send with the least amount of money. Simply add the lightest items first and then add the heavier items until you have reached your budget! This way, you can get more items in one go!

Tip 5: Sign Up for Loyalty Programs and Newsletters!

If you are an avid and frequent online shopper, you may have come across or signed up to some form of loyalty program or newsletter for a site. Many online retailers across the world use these systems to provide their customers with exclusive content as well as attracting new customers.

A newsletter membership or system is common among most websites. The site usually will have a place where the user can request emails that contain exclusive offers and updates about the products and websites. This means that the user provides the site with an email address. They will then receive one or more emails throughout the week. The contents of the emails vary depending on the provide, however, they usually contain exclusive offers, sales, and even discounts for the people who have signed up to the newsletter system.

Some websites also offer their members some form of loyalty system. These types of websites change depending on what goods they are selling as well as the popularity of the store. Many smaller shops that sell specialty goods, such as K-pop, usually have a loyalty system in place. The systems vary from site to site, but it is common for the loyalty system to be either digital cash or point based. The process is quite simple. Simply sign up to the website using your real information and then make a purchase. A percentage of the purchase will be "refunded" in the form of digital points or cash. You can then use the points or cash to get discounts on your next purchase. This is only one of the many loyalty systems out there, but it is the most common and popular system to use on K-Pop based websites.

Finding a website that offers these sorts of benefits, can be extremely helpful. Although you will not receive rewards instantly, over time, you will gain many different types of discounts and benefits compared to the average buyer. Finding a K-Pop website that has these sorts of systems isn't too hard, simply look around and you are bound to find something that suits you!

Save Money by Buying Through Group Orders

Buying K-Pop goods can be extremely expensive and sometimes it's simply just not worth the price. To combat the increasingly rising shipping fees, fans came up with a way to make the fees cheaper. The answer? Group orders! A group order is when a group of people purchase many items in one transaction for the sole purpose of reducing the cost of shipping. Buying as a group has two main benefits. Firstly, if a group order has enough orders, they can potentially purchase their albums in bulk, which in some cases can mean that the transaction will be discounted. However, the main benefit is that the shipping fee is split by everyone who ordered, making it cheaper for everyone!

A group is typically organised and run by an individual or a small group of people. The person who oversees the group order will more than likely have some form of supplier. There are many different types of suppliers. The first supplier is the official website that sells and distributes merchandise

A group order can be run by an individual or a small group. The person who is running the order, the leader, will more than likely have a supplier. A supplier can either be an official website or third-party website that stocks and sells the item in interest, or it can be a person who is currently residing in the area where the item is being sold. There are also some cases where the person who is running the group order is either living in South Korea or near a place where the merchandise is being sold and is willing to send the items internationally. There are also some group orders that are run by people who are holidaying or visiting South Korea and are willing to bring back the items to their own country.

What is the Process of a Group Order?

The process of a group order can take some time; however, it is incredibly simple. Although group orders will vary depending on who is running the order, group orders will more than likely have a form that the buyer is required to fill out. The form serves two purposes. Firstly, to outline the rules and process of the group order. As well as collect the information the group order leader will need regarding the item you are buying, your payment details, address and any other important information the buyer should know.

After you have read the form and agreed to the terms and conditions you can then fill it out and place an order. In most cases you will be required to pay for the items before a certain deadline. If you fail to pay, the order will not go through and you will more than likely be blacklisted from any future group orders from that person. It is extremely important when paying for items that you make sure that you protect your banking details! Most group orders will give you the option of using either PayPal or bank transfer to pay for you groups. PayPal is the safer option as you won't be giving them your banking details and you can file claims against the receiver if by chance you never receive your items.

Once the deadline is reached and all payments have been received, the leader will then go ahead and place the order for the merchandise. As the products are most likely coming from South Korea, the items can easily take over 2 - 4 weeks to arrive. Be aware if you are purchasing goods that are yet to be released (pre-ordering) or buying signed merchandise, it can take more time. Many people who purchase signed merchandise do not receive their items until a couple of months after the release date. After the items are received by the leader, they will either make an announcement or contact you directly stating that they have received the items.

After that, all that is left is to collect your items. Group orders will typically offer two ways to receive your items, postage or meetups. Postage simply means that the leader will post the items to you directly (at your own cost). Be aware that by choosing shipping, it is possible that your album could become lost or damaged in the process. As for meetups, meetups are when the leader arranges a date and place where they will meet you either individually or as a group (everyone who ordered) to collect the items. Individual meetups are usually only arranged when only a small number of albums were purchased. If you do arrange to individually meetup to collect your items, it is suggested that you go with a friend or family member to collect your items (if you are underage). You should never attend a meetup by yourself unless you personally know the person who is running it.

Where can I Find a Group Order?

For someone who has never joined a group order before, finding one can be extremely difficult. However, due to the increasingly popularity and interest in K-Pop merchandise, group orders are becoming more accessible and easier to find. Most group orders are typically run through some form of social media. The most common platforms are twitter, Facebook and Tumblr.

Finding a group order will differ depending on the social media platform you use. If you are planning on finding a Facebook based group order, try searching through communities and groups that are for selling and trading K-Pop merchandise. Many group order leaders will advertise their own groups that are dedicated for group orders via these communities. Also look for groups that are for a specific are or band. Many people will post group orders that are limited to certain countries, so join as many K-Pop related groups (that are run by fans!!!) as you can.

Twitter and Tumblr use similar searching features such as hashtags. When searching for a group order, try searching hash tags that will relate to the merchandise you are wanting to order. E.g. the name of the merchandise, #GroupOrder #Yourcountry #The band name etc. Another way is to follow any fan sites or fans that you may have come across on these platforms. If you are lucky, one of the fan sites will either share or run their own group order (which isn't uncommon).

Please be aware that just like ordering anything off the internet, there is a possibility that you could potentially be scammed or ripped off. Trying to figure out whether a group order is legit or not is extremely hard to spot. Although you can never be certain, there are a few ways you can check the legitimacy of the group order. Firstly, make sure to check whether the person running the group order has previously run a group order or whether people have complained about the person before. If you think the prices are too high, make sure to look around at other group orders and online websites. The biggest tip is to pay via PayPal! That way if you do NOT receive your items, you can make a claim against the seller and hopefully get your money back!

Second Hand Merchandise

Second hand merchandise is probably one of the most common ways to purchase K-Pop merchandise. Many fans, especially younger fans, cannot afford to buy brand new merchandise as soon as it comes out, as such, many K-Pop fans turn to buying their goods second hand. And honestly, there is nothing wrong with that!

There are two main ways you can buy second hand merchandise, either online or offline. Of course, finding merchandise offline in non-Asian countries is going to be a ton hard than in Asia. So, it isn't unusual for many international fans to purchase their second-hand merchandise online.

With the rising popularity of K-Pop on social media such as Facebook, Twitter and Instagram, many people buy, sell and trade their merchandise on these platforms! There are also many online sites that allow their users to list and sell their merchandise either for a small fee or free. One of the most well-known sites for this is eBay! Users can list and sell their items for a small fee and the buyers can see multiple listings for the items they are seeking. Although K-pop is quite popular there are not many people who use eBay to sell. Instead, a newer application called Carousel, is becoming a popular way to sell K-pop merchandise! Many people also sell their second-hand goods on their personal or selling group pages. There are many K-Pop groups on Facebook that are dedicated to buying, selling and swapping K-Pop merchandise, so you shouldn't have any trouble finding where to buy second hand goods.

Buying second hand merchandise is an extremely good idea if you are running low on funds! However, you need to be aware that by buying second hand goods, you will not be directly supporting your artists. By buying second hand, all the money will be going to the original owner instead of the artists, so if you are wanting to support your artists directly, try saving up some fund before you make a purchase. If you have no problem with this, then go ahead! There are many K-Pop fans who buy their merchandise second hand, so no one will judge!

One thing to be aware of, is that you will always be at risk of being scammed when purchasing second hand goods. You never know who the person is and there is a chance that you may either receive extremely damaged goods or not receive the items at all! Always do your research before you make any transaction. Be aware that even if they are listed on websites such as Amazon or eBay, it does not guarantee that the products are authentic, or it is not a scam. There are still many people who run these types of scams and you could possibly be their next victim!

Chapter 8: Staying Safe from Scams!

No matter who you are or what your buying, nobody wants to get scammed. The easiest way to prevent yourself from potentially being scammed is to either buy your goods from physical stores or by purchasing through official websites such as the entertainment agencies! However, at times, buying merchandise from official vendors can be extremely expensive, so many people decide to purchase their goods second hand or through group orders.

Types of Scams

Type 1: Fake Merchandise & Albums

K-Pop being a music industry, sell millions of albums both internationally and nationally. As such, there are many people who wish to take advantage of the increasing popularity of K-Pop. Many people around the world mass produce fake merchandise such as photocards, albums and even clothing lines! This is one of the most common types of scams among online retailers who claim to be selling official merchandise.

Fake merchandise in the K-pop community is becoming a more frequent event and there are many people who are being scammed. One of the most common types of fake merchandise being sold is photocards and signed albums. These two are common due to one reason, they can be easily produced. All you need to make a fake signed album is some good handwriting and a marker. As for photocards, there are hundreds of different tutorials and methods for making them, so it isn't hard at all.

In some cases, the albums will be official, but the signatures of idols are forged. There is no real way to identify whether a signature is forged or not, and the best way to find out is by asking for some form of proof such as a receipt. Most signed albums that are owned by international fans are acquired via Mwave. Mwave is an official site and store that sells signed and limited items to K-Pop fans around the world. Just liked any store, the person who purchased the item should have some form of proof. You should also compare the albums signatures to the idols signatures (That can be easily found on the internet).

Compared to signed albums, fake photocards are a lot easier to spot! When seeing whether a photocard is fake or not, you should look at the size, texture and colours of the photocards. Most fake photocards with have discoloration on the back of the cards and will be made from a different material. The only hard part about spotting fake photocards, is that it is extremely hard to notice the texture, size and discoloration via a computer screen. As such, it is recommended that you only purchase or trade photo cards in person rather than online. The only exception would be if you have purchased from the person multiple times or now the seller personally.

If you can't meet with the person as the distance is too far, you should always check to see if there have been previous buyers from the seller. Ask them a few questions such as did they receive their item? Was it damaged? Etc. If they have sold multiple items before, it is safer than buying from someone who has never sold anything!

Type 2: Paying & Not Receiving

Many people fall victim to this type of scam and no matter how much you pay, it's always an awful feeling knowing that you have been scammed. Buying K-pop merchandise and albums can be extremely expensive as it is, being scammed does not help. If you are an international fan, chances are being that you are trying to buy a second-hand item from your country. In most cases you will have to pay postage to receive the goods. However, be extremely careful when buying from another seller. There have been many incidents of people paying for an item and then not receiving them or losing contact with the seller.

If you plan to buy from another seller, make sure you look at the persons profile and ask many questions to both the seller and the community. If the seller has more positive feedback, chances are they are legit. If the seller is new, you will have to judge whether they are legit purely from the conversation that you have as well as the information and photos you receive. However, just because the seller seems confident and nice, doesn't necessarily mean that they are a legit seller! Some scammers also usually only use one photo which can be easily sourced from anywhere on the internet. If you ask for more photos and they are willing to do so, it will add a bit more assurance that they do have the physical album.

Buying merchandise second is a good idea, if you do a lot of research and seek feedback from other buyers. It someone is selling for the first time, it is difficult to tell if they are a legit seller. So, make sure to ask many questions and request many photos of the items.

Type 3: Paying too much & Shipping Scamming!

Before you go ahead and purchase a second-hand album or an album from an online store, you should check the price on the official website! This way you will know the exact price of the album. Most K-Pop albums range from $15 - $35 for normal albums. Special, limited edition, signed, or albums that are no longer being produced, tend to sell for a higher price, after all, they are rarer than your typical albums. If a second-hand album is over $30, you will want to see what condition the album is, the age as well as whether that price includes shipping. If not, you may want to try negotiating or look elsewhere. Some online retailers are usually cheap, but you may pay an arm and leg for shipping! Check the shipping rates of multiple stores before you buy!

Here is where this type of scam gets difficult to judge when buying second hand items. Some sellers try to scam you and blame it on shipping! Shipping fees can be incredibly high, but sometimes people bump up the prices, so they can make a bigger profit. The best thing to do to see if you are getting shipping scammed, is to ask who the seller will be sending it through, where they are sending it from and what service they are using (E.g. tracking services, airmail, express shipping etc). This way you can do the maths yourself by going on to the postage services. It also helps if you ask for photos of the merchandise, so you can see the exact weight, as well as proof of the dimensions of the box. There are going to be sellers who refuse, but those who are legit are more likely to provide proof!

Chapter 9: Storing & Protecting Merchandise

As a K-pop fan, chances are you have already acquainted yourself with the almighty cost of owning K-Pop related merchandise! The fees and costs can be extremely high, and you do not want that money to go to waste. One of the most common questions for merchandise, is how to store and protect your merchandise without damaging it. There are many ways that you can protect your items will still displaying it. There are three main types of merchandise that K-Pop fans typically have. That is K-Pop albums, posters and photocards. This is because all three can typically be bought together and come with a specific album.

Before you start displaying your favourite posters or stacking your albums on a shelf. There are a few things you are going to want to know beforehand. These are common mistakes that are made on a regular basis. The following will tell you some tips for storage as well as what you could potentially be doing to your merchandise if you don't look after and display them right!

Protecting Albums

Tip 1: Avoid Stacking your Albums!

If you are living in a small apartment or simply don't have any space to store your albums, you may come up with the "smart" idea of stacking albums on top of each other. Although it may sound like a brilliant idea to save shelf space, it is one of the worst things you could do to your albums. Without even realizing it, your albums could be getting severely damaged. There may not be any noticeable damages on the outside, however, chances are that the internal content of the album is or will be damaged. This not only affects the quality and condition of the album, but if you have intentions to sell it down the road, it could affect the selling price.

In every album there is obviously going to be a disk, and where there is a disk there will be a disk holder. Most disk holders are made of a hard plastic and are usually positioned on the opposite side of the photobook. If you were to stack albums on top of each other, the weight would compress the album. In most albums, this will cause the disk plate to firmly press against the photobook, causing damages such as indents, scratches and tears.

There are a few exceptions where it would be ok to stack albums on top of each other. The first exception is when the album comes in a box or a clear plastic case. Japanese albums are typically packaged like American albums and are stored in clear plastic cases, making it safe to stack them. Albums that are packaged in boxes can also be stacked as they have a solid case and can withstand pressure. However, it's still recommended that you don't stack boxed albums as they may sink in the centre over time.

The best way of storing albums is to place them side by side like books. Have the spine of the album facing outwards and make sure the there is some pressure (not too much) against the albums. Just enough to keep them firmly closed without causing any damage. As stated above, albums that are in a clear plastic case can be stacked to save room as well as albums that come in boxes.

Tip 2: Plate & Book Holders are your Best Friend!

Signed albums are extremely popular among both Korean and international fans of K-pop. However, when you receive the album, you are going to want to show off the fact that you have a signed album right? Well the easiest way to do this is by investing in something even your grandma may own, a plate holder. If you have ever been to a home of the older generation such as your grandparents, it is possible that they have decorative plates on display. Although the plate may be interesting, you should be more interested in the holder in which it is resting on. The plate holders are a great way to safely display the albums without damaging them. They also come in many different fancy designs, colours and sizes; so, finding one to suit your album shouldn't be too hard. They are also reasonably cheap and can be found at most dollar stores!

If you cannot find a plate holder, try searching for book holders instead. If you don't know what they are, you can easily go to your local library! They are almost identical to plate holders, although they may be slightly different in design. Some plate holders firmly hold the plate; however, a book holder simply acts as a stand / rest, meaning it does not hold it firmly in place.

Tip 3: Protect the Corners!

One of the most common forms of damage on an album, is the bending and tearing of corners. Protecting the corners of albums is one of the hardest things to do in terms of protecting your albums. Albums come in many different sizes and shapes, as such, there are many albums that do not come in a solid box. Many albums are designed like a book, so, just like a book, it is common for the corners to become bent and damaged over time. The easiest way to protect the corners of an album is to make sure that the albums are stored with the spine facing outwards and for the albums to be slightly compressed against each other. This ensures that the album has no free space to move around and it will stop the pages of the photobook from rubbing against the shelf.

Another way to protect the corners of an album is by investing or making a corner protector. If you have ever bought a brand-new picture frame or canvas, you may have come across think triangle shaped pieces of cardboard on the corners of the product. These are used to prevent the corners from becoming damaged while resting on the shelves. The protectors are easy to make and can be made from many different types of material from fabric to plastic. However, it is recommended that they are made of a hard material. If you want to just buy them, they are typically called Book Corner Protectors. They are commonly being made of metal. One thing to be aware of when buying them, is that it could possibly scratch the album, or the protectors may require digging in slightly to the album, which could potentially leave dents in the album.

Tip 4: Where to Store Albums!

Whether it is intentional or not, many K-Pop fans who collect albums like to display their collections. Chances are, if you are starting your collection, you will need to sort out a place where you are going to store them. The most common way is by simply storing them in a bookcase. Since albums are designed either like a book or in a smallish box, a bookshelf is one of the easiest and safest way to store them. Bookshelves provide the perfect place for displaying albums safely, without causing any harm to them. Bookshelves do range in price and can be expensive at times. However, if you are tight on money, you can always buy a second hand one and either make it pretty yourself or buy a better one in the future.

The biggest and most common problem with bookshelves is that they can take about a lot of space. So, if you don't have a lot of room in your home or you are lacking the funds a bookshelf, you have two basic options. Firstly, you can settle for a smaller bookshelf or drawers. If you are starting your collection, you are probably not going to need a whole bookshelf. So maybe settle with a small storage cube or set of draws. The other option is to invest in hard plastic storage containers. Storage containers are the better option if you have limited space as they can be stored in places such as under your bed or in the closet! They are also reasonably cheap! The only thing you must consider, is that over time the container could become extremely heavy as albums aren't as light as they seem. You also must make sure to never stack albums on top of each other!

If all else fails, you can also store your albums anywhere that has a solid surface! Never store albums on soft surfaces such as on carpets or fabrics. Storing them on such surfaces increases the chances of the edges and corners of the albums to become bent and torn. Simply resting them on a table top or bench will work perfectly until you find a better place! If you have a spare shelf somewhere, then that is an even better option!

Protecting Photocards

Tip 1: Card Sleeves

One of the most popular ways to store, protect and display photocards is using card sleeves. If you are a fan of trading card games such as Pokémon or Yu Gi Oh, you have probably come across or heard of card sleeves before. Card sleeves are made of a thin plastic that are designed to protect and store various types of trading cards. The card sleeves were originally designed to protect and store both trading card games and baseball cards. However, they can be used to store K-Pop photocards as well!

There are many different types of card sleeves that come in different shapes, sizes and colours. The most common among K-Pop fans, is the standard nine pocket card sleeve. The card sleeves are designed to fit into most two or three ring binders. Since most sheets are made of a clear plastic, both the front and back of the photocards can be easily seen. Photocards can also be put back to back to save more space, meaning that each sheet can potentially hold a total of 18 cards! Depending on the quality of brand you buy, depends on the strength of the plastic.

A popular brand amongst both trading card and K-Pop fanatics, is a brand called UltraPro. UltraPro produce a wide range of products in card protection and trading. The standard nine pocket card sleeve is the same size as a standard deck of cards. Occasionally you will also come across photocards that are like a postcard or larger in size. Not to fear though! Ultra pro offers a wide range of different size card sleeves that have larger sized pockets! If you only have a few photocards and don't wish to purchase a binder and sleeves, the sleeves are also sold as individual pockets that can hold one card at a time!

Card sleeves are relatively easy to find if you know where to look! As the sleeves are designed specifically for trading card games, the sleeves can be easily found at game and speciality stores! There are also many online stores and retailers that stock and sell different types of card sleeves. One of the best places to look is on sites such as Amazon or eBay, as you can often buy in bulk or with discounts.

If you plan to purchase protective card sleeves, you need to be aware that although you are protecting the edges of the cards and they can be easily displayed, cards in the sleeves can still become damaged. Since the sleeves are made of a thin plastic, if they are not protected by a hard binder, the cards can potentially be dented! Card sleeves also have a habit of slowly bending you card as the plastic is not thick! However, the simple solution is to simply put a thicker sheet of plastic or cardboard in the pocket alongside your photocard This will protect it from bending and make sure that the card remains flat.

Tip 2: Top Loaders

Top loaders are like the father of card protectors! They are strong, sturdy and get the job done. Just like card sleeves, top loaders are made of a plastic material! The only difference is that a top loader is made of a thicker and stronger kind of plastic. The only downside is that top loaders are only sold in individual pockets as it would be too hard to manipulate the plastic for 9 sleeve pockets. Top loaders are also more expensive than normal card sleeves, however, they do offer more support and protection to the photocards. If you have quite a few photocards, card sleeves are probably the better way to go!

Top loaders are also a great way to protect photo cards if you are sending or trading them with some via mail. We all know how dodgy the mail service can be, so the thicker the material of the protector, the better chances your photocard has of surviving! They can also make the photocards waterproof. If you place a photocard inside the protector and place a piece of sticky tape over the top edge, the card has a better chance of surviving if it rains!

Top loaders are perfect for people who do not have a lot of storage in their homes. Unlike card sleeves that must be placed in a large binder, Top loaders can be stored practically everywhere. Since they are smaller in size and made of a thicker material, the protectors can be stacked on top of each other or fit in small areas, so it's a great way to store photocards while saving space.

If you are planning to purchase top loaders, you need to be aware of a few things. Firstly, top loaders are only available as single pockets. There is no such thing as a nine-sleeve top loader sheet! So, if you have many photocard, it would be cheaper and easier to buy the normal nine sleeve pockets. Secondly, top loaders are extremely hard to find in physical stores. Your chances of finding them are slim! But if you have no problem with internet shopping, then you should have no problem with finding them! Finally, top loaders typically only come in one size! Finding sizes that are larger than the typical deck of cards, can be extremely difficult to find, even on online stores! So, if you have larger photocards, you may need to find another option for protecting and storing them!

Tip 3: Photo Albums

Another inexpensive way to store photocards is by using photo albums. Photo albums come in a wide range of different colours, shapes and sizes and are widely accessible on both online and physical stores. So, finding a photo album that suits your taste and purchase shouldn't be too hard to find! They can also be reasonably cheap, so if you are on a tight budget, you should really consider buying one!

The main benefit of using a photo album is that it can store larger size photo cards. Occasionally you are going to come across photocards that are the same size as postcards or larger, which can be an absolute pain to store and protect! These types of cards don't usually fit into your average card sleeves, but they will fit perfectly in a photo album!

There are a few concerns with using photo albums. Firstly, the cards can potentially become damaged. The cards are protected by a sleeve; however, this will not prevent the cards from bending over time. Just like the card sleeves, it's recommended that you put a thin sleeve of cardboard in alongside the photo card. Some photo albums also do not have a clear back. If you are wanting to see both the back and front of the card, you are going to have to look around for a photo album that provides a clear backing.

Tip 4: Photo Frames

Protecting merchandise with photo frames in more common when displaying posters, however, you can also protect and store photocards in them! Not many people consider using photo frames to protect their photocards, yet, it is one of the best ways to display them.

Photo frames are a great for two main reasons. Firstly, the photocard is extremely protected. A photo frame has both a backing and a clear front plate, meaning the photocard will be compressed between the front and back. This not only stops the card from sliding around, but it also protects it from getting scratches. The cards edges will remain in a perfect condition and there is no way for the card to bend or tear. The frame also offers so water protection and depending what frame you buy, it can also protect the card from fading over time. Secondly, they are the perfect way to show off and display your cards out in the open! Photo frames can practically rest anywhere and since they can be small, you have the option of either resting it on a hard surface or hanging it up on a wall without causing any damage!

One of the main benefits of choosing a photo frame, is that they are easily accessible and easy to find. Most if not all homeware stores will have some type of photo frame. You can even get giant wall frames that hold multiple photos in cute patterns. They also come in many different shapes and sizes, which gives you more customization options. There are also many online retailers that offer and provide custom frames that are created based off your measurements.

Just like any method of protecting photo cards, there are also a few negatives. Firstly, photo frames can take up a ton of space People with limited storage areas may have difficulty displaying the frames. In the same respect, they can also be hung up, meaning you aren't taking up much space at all. The other problem is that it can be extremely expensive if you have a lot of photocards. If you only have a few photocards, then go ahead and display them! However, if you are an avid collector (or plan to be) you may want to consider only buying 2 or 3 frames to display your favourite or rare photocards and buy card sleeves for the remainder.

Tip 5: Keep them in the Album!

After buying you first ever album, you probably don't have anywhere to store the Photocards that are included. If you are looking for a simple and cheap way to keep the cards well protected, the easiest way to do so, is by leaving inside the albums that they came from. In most cases, the photocards will typically be found in the photobook that came with the album. Photocards are usually found towards the back or middle of the photobooks and are usually wedged between the pages or spine. The photocards are kept inside of the albums until they are bought by someone. Obviously if they aren't damaged when you receive them, it is a pretty good way to store them. If you simply leave the photocard where you found it, the chances of it becoming damaged in some way, are slim.

Another reason why you should leave the photocard in the photobook is because photocards can bend! The material of photocards can vary and depending on how you store it, the cards can start to curve and bend over time. Storing it inside a photobook, compresses the photocard and will keep it straight. It will also protect the card from any potential scratches or tears. If you do plan to store the photocard in the photobook, you need to ensure that the photocard is positioned in the middle of the page and not resting at the base of the photobook. There may not be any noticeable damages or threats to begin with, however, over time the edges and corners of the photocard can become damaged due to the rubbing against the surface in which you store it. Another tip is to make sure you store the photocard, so it is resting firmly against the spine of the photobook. Most photocards are usually stored this way before the albums have been purchased. The reason for doing this is that if you store the photocard so it is resting against the spine, it will grip the photocard when you close the book, stopping the card from sliding around inside the album! It will also help protect the edges and corners from damage.

As there are many different types of albums, there is never a guarantee that the photocard will be stored inside the photobook. Depending on how the albums is designed or what is included in the album, the photocard can be found in several different places. If a photocard isn't found inside a photobook, chances are there is a reason behind it! If you purchase an album where the photocard is stored separately from the photobook, simply leave it where it is found. Of course, you can move it depending on whether you believe the card will become damaged or bent.

Protecting Posters

K-pop fans that live outside of South Korea or an Asian Country, will more than likely be purchasing their K-pop merchandise from an online retailer. If this is the case, chances are being that you are going to come across posters at some point. When purchasing K-pop merchandise, more specifically albums; many artists include posters. In most cases, posters are usually included as part of the pre-order or first press benefit. However, there are also posters that come with all albums or can be bought separately. Although receiving posters can be exciting, it makes the shipping process a nightmare.

When buying from online retailers and official websites, many retailers will provide the buyer with the option of have the poster sent folded or rolled up in a protective tube. To save money, most fans make the simple mistake of choosing to get their posters sent folded. Although having the poster sent folded is free, you are basically spending your money on a damaged product. If you are assuming your poster will make it safely to your house folded, is a big mistake. You never know what can happen during the shipping process, your poster can and will more than likely become damaged in some way shape or form. Without the extra protection, the poster can easily become water damaged or torn during the shipping process! Not only that, if you purchase multiple items, it's likely that the poster will be compressed between larger and heavier items. Over time, the compression of the poster can cause defined creases throughout the poster where it was folded. The creases will make the poster weaker and will increase its chances of becoming torn in the future. Defined creases can also cause the poster to lose its colors in the areas in which it is folded, causing it to have white patches in the middle (which is the last thing any K-pop fan wants!).

Although getting a poster folded is free, you are better off having the poster sent in a protective tube and pay an additional fee. The price of a protective tube varies depending on the retailer, however, the average price is between $3 - $6. In most cases, you will only need to purchase one poster tube and they will pack all your posters in the one tube. Buying a poster tube does not guarantee that the poster will not get damaged in some way, however, it will increase its chances of arriving safely and undamaged. Poster tubes are commonly made of either thicker and sturdier material such as thick cardboard or plastic. This means that even if the box was to become damaged in some way, such as becoming torn or wet during the shipping process; the posters have an added layer of protection that could potentially protect them. Having a poster sent in a poster tube also means that the poster will not need to be folded, instead, it will be rolled up in the tube. This means that there will not be any creases in the poster and it will not be as weak as it would if it was folded. Poster tubes also provide you with a safe place to store unused posters over long periods of time, making them the perfect option if you have limited storage place. The quality of the poster would remain in a great condition which is extremely important if you decide to sell them in the future!

Whether you choose to get a poster sent folded or in a poster tube, your next problem is where and how can you display it without damaging it. Here are a few tips to help you out!

Tip 1: Purchase a Picture Frame

One of the biggest problems about posters, is that if you don't display it correctly, you are more than likely going to damage it. When you receive a poster, you are probably wondering how you can display it for a long period of time! The best solution is to invest in a good quality picture frame. Although this may seem a little overboard, a picture frame is one of the best ways to display a poster! Storing a poster in a picture frame will provide the poster with extra protection against potential threats that could damage the poster over time. This could include dust, light and even water! One of the major problems with posters, are that they are commonly made of a thin paper material. Posters made of a thin material are prone to tears and rips, thus it is extremely important to protect them as much as you can. There are many different types of paper such as matte, gloss and canvas, however, no matter how strong or thick the material is, paper will always have one major enemy, water! You shouldn't have to worry about water damage too much, however, there is still a chance that the poster could be water damaged. A picture frame can prevent a poster from potentially becoming damaged as it is encased in a glass or plastic frame that compressed the poster between a strong and thick backing, making it near impossible from the poster to tear and minimizing the chances of it becoming water damaged. Some expensive frames also offer extra benefits such as reflective glass and fade protection!

Using a photo frame is one of the best ways to protect posters over long periods of time, however, it is also one of the most expensive ways in which you can store them. There is no set size for a K-pop poster, meaning that there may be times in which finding a frame for a poster can prove to be impossible, which is extremely common among larger posters. In some cases, it is possible that you may be required to purchase a custom-made photo frame which can be quite pricey! The price can also accumulate over time. If you need to buy several different sized photo frames for several different posters, the prices could be quite shocking. As such, try looking around your local second-hand shops and on online retailers before you head out shipping!

Another problem with picture frames is that finding a place to hang them can post as a problem for those who are renting or don't wish to damage the walls of their home. If you are one of these unfortunate people, you are in luck. If drilling a hole or hammering a nail into the wall is out of the question, there is always the option of purchasing removable hooks. Removable hooks come in various sizes, colors and shapes, making it a perfect alternative to permanent hooks. When purchasing removable hooks, it is important that you know how heavy the picture frame is. It is extremely important that you weigh the frame before purchasing, as most removable hooks have weight limits. If you want to make sure that your frame won't come crashing down in a matter of seconds, make sure you check the weight of your frame and the weight in which the hook can hold! Also make sure to check the back of your picture frame to see how the frame can be hung. Every frame will have a different design and it is important to check before buying as it is possible that the hook may not even fit the frame! Finally, check the surface in which you are hanging it. Make sure to have a place in mind before you go out and buy removable hooks as there are some hooks that are designed for certain surfaces that can cause problems if you hang them in the wrong spot!

Tip 2: Avoid Blu Tack and Thumbtacks

Blu Tack and Thumbtacks are two of the most popular tools used by K-pop fans to display and hang their posters. Why? Because Blu Tack and Thumbtacks are two of the simplest, easiest and affordable ways in which you could hang a poster. However, every product has its faults and many K-pop fans do not know about the damages that Blu Tack and Thumb Tacks can cause to their posters over time.

Using a thumbtack on anything is going to do obvious and noticeable harm to the product, after all, you are sticking a needle / pin into your poster. But thumbtacks don't only damage your poster, it also damages the surface in which you are pinning it to. Unless you are pinning it to a cork board, there will always be traces in the form of a small hole, of where you have hung posters. Although thumbtacks aren't as common as using Blu tack, many people still choose to use them when displaying their poster. Of course, thumb tacks do have their own benefits though. Luckily, they are cheap, so if you have many posters to hang, it isn't going to cost you a fortune. And unlike Blu Tack, if you drop it on carpet, you will not struggle to get it out, if you can find the thumbtack and don't stand on it, you shouldn't have a problem. The main problem with Thumbtacks is that they require you to pierce the poster to hang it, aka you are damaging the poster! If you don't mind damaging your poster slightly, then all means use them. However, if you want to keep them in mint condition, you are better off looking for an alternative!

As for Blu Tack, it is one of the biggest and most popular poster killers! Blu Tack is the most common way to display posters and although there may not be any noticeable damages to the poster as soon as you hang it up, Blu tack will more than likely damage your poster over time. Over time, the blue tack will start to leave an oil stain on the poster. Although it does take a while for the oil from the blue tack to leach into the poster, once it is there, there is no way in which it can be removed. The oil stain can cause the material to become thin and potentially break, but it can also cause noticeable discoloration on both the front and back of the poster.

Just like thumbtacks, Blu Tack can also damage your walls if it stays on them for long periods of time. Over time the oil can either leach into the paint on the walls and cause the paint to peel or stain. The Blu tack can also harden, making it extremely hard to remove and could potentially chip the paint where it was hanging.

If you have no other option than to use Blu Tack or simply just wish to use it, there are a few ways you can protect both your walls and posters from being damaged. Firstly, Blu Tack can come in many different colours. Although you may not be able to find the exact match to you walls, try buying a colour that is as close as possible. If you can't find coloured Blu tack, you should always go with white as there is no added colouring! This will prevent any colour stains on the paint, especially if you buy cheap or knock off brands. As for protecting your poster, make sure that you change the location of the Blu Tack every couple of weeks. This will reduce the chances of the Blu Tack from leaving an oil stain on the poster. It will also stop the Blu Tack from stiffening which could cause the paint to peel off the walls if you try to remove it.

If you need a cheaper alternative then picture frames, but a safer option than Blu tack or thumbtacks, then poster / glue dots are the way to go. Poster dots are specifically designed for hanging up posters while being safe and easy to remove. Although they can be peeled off easy, they stick firmly to the wall without peeling off. The only problem with poster dots, is that if you live in an area that reaches extremely hot temperatures, it is possible for the dots to peel off either the wall or poster. If this happens it may be better to find an alternative, however, you can always just replace them! Poster dots can be found in most stationary or craft stores! If you can't find them, you can always find them online. Although poster dots are a little more expensive compared to Blu tack and thumbtacks, they are a safer and more reliable way to protect your posters and walls.

Tip 3: Avoid Direct Sunlight

Discoloration and fading in posters are bound to happen over time, however, you can reduce the chances of it fading faster. Of course, you are going to want to show it off and display it somewhere where is will be seen on a regular basis. However, what you don't want to do is display the poster in a place that frequently gets direct sunlight. Why? Well it's simple, if you hang your poster in direct sunlight for long periods of time, over time the colours will begin to fade, and the paper could potentially become frail.

To avoid damaging the poster from the sun, simply display the poster in an area in which there is little to no direct sunlight, although it isn't necessary to block out all sunlight, try to keep it to a minimum. The best places to hang a poster is on the walls in hallways, next to windows (as oppose to opposite the window), on the back of doors as well as any other dark place. The places you want to try to avoid are directly opposite windows and directly on windows (Yes, people do hang posters on windows).

Chapter 10: The K-Pop Dictionary

Fitting into the K-pop community can be hard, but it is even harder to understand some of the terms that K-pop fans use when referring to different aspects of K-pop. This could be phrases or words that are slang or simple Korean fans that international fans use on a regular basis. Below are words that are commonly used in the K-pop community, in both South Korea and internationally.

4D - The term 4D usually refers to the personality of an Idol. Being considered 4D is usually when an idol behaves and acts differently or strangely compared to the usual Korean standards. There are many 4D idols that are well known such as Lee Jaejin from Sechskies and V from BTS.

Aegyo - Aegyo is when someone acts excessively cute. This can be done through many ways such as doing "Cute" voices or actions. Aegyo is usually used when doing fanservice, however, there are many idols who have natural aegyo / are naturally cute.

All Kill - When artists release albums, their songs and albums are usually ranked on a music chart. An all kill is when an album or song tops all music charts.

Anti-Fan - An anti-fan is the opposite of a fan. Instead of liking and supporting an artist, they despise and try to an artist's career and reputation. Anti-fans are usually the starters of negative rumors, scandals and gossip about the artist. They also tend to attack the artists and their fans. This can be achieved either by leaving negative comments about the artist on social media and attacking fans and the artist physically as well as verbally. Anti-fans are usually well known in the fandoms and they commonly know more information about the artist they hate than some actual fans of the artist.

Bias - A bias is a member of a group in which you feel a stronger attraction to when compared to the other members of the group. Most people have one bias per group.

Ultimate Bias - Just like a Bias, an Ultimate Bias is your all-time favourite member or artist from all groups that you follow and is considered your #1 artist.

Bias Wrecker - A member of a group that continuously catches your attention. A Bias Wrecker is a member you tend to start following and makes you question whether they are your bias or not (Even though you already have a bias).

The Big 3 - The Big 3 is the nickname given to the three largest entertainment agencies within South Korea. The Big 3 consists of SM entertainment, JYP Entertainment and YG Entertainment.

Bong - A bong is another world for a light stick which is like a specially designed torch that is commonly used during fan meetings, concerts and official events. Many artists (especially groups) have their own bongs.

Comeback - When an artist releases a new album after their previous promotional activities were completed.

Fan café - An official website that is typically run by the management of the artist. They are slowly becoming uncommon among K-pop artists and are more common in older groups. The website is used by both fans and the artist to communicate and be up to date with schedules, news and release of official content. A Fan café is usually formatted like an online forum.

Debut - A debut is when an artist performs and releases their own content such as an album for the first time. Once they debut, they are no longer considered a trainee.

Fan chant - A chant, Rhyme or song that fans sing and shout during live performances such as music shows, concerts and other official events. The chant typically incorporates all the names of the artists and can also include the name of the group and the album in which they are promoting.

Fan Club - A club for the fans of an artist. A Fan club can either an unofficial club run by fans or an official club that is run by the entertainment agency of the artist.

Fan Meeting - An official event in which artists and fans get to interact one a more personal level. K-pop groups and artists typically sit along a table and fans get to individually meet and greet the members in one on one interactions. There are also fan meetings in which it is held like a concert (without the performances) and are just talking and playing games with fans as a group.

Fan Service - Fan service is when an artist completes requests of the fans or does specific actions to please their fans. This could include but is not limited to, acting cute, making hearts, acting and more.

Fan War - When fans of two separate artists or groups fight and attack each other's artists and fans. A fan war can be caused due to the competitive atmosphere of music charts and award shows.

Fandom - A group of people who follow and support the same artist and group. There is a separate fandom for each artist and group.

Fan Site - An unofficial site that is typically run by a fan of an artist. The contents of the site can vary from pictures and videos of the artist; to news and information relating to the artists schedules, albums, merchandise and official events.

First press - Merchandise that was produced during the first mass production of the merchandise. Receiving a first press item is almost guaranteed when merchandise is pro-ordered. First press merchandise sometimes comes with special gifts or benefits such as polaroid pictures, posters, photo cards etc.

Fighting! - The term is meant to encourage someone and can be a word for "You can do it!". It is a common word among by fans and artists alike.

Hallyu - The Hallyu wave or the Korean Wave, is a term used to refer to the mass spread and rising popularity of Korean culture and entertainment on a global scale.

Hyung - Hyung is the Korean word meaning older brother. It is a common word used by many Koreans and can be used to refer to both your biological brother, as well as a close older male friend, as such, it is common for younger members of a group to refer to the older members as Hyung.

Maknae - The Maknae is the youngest member in a group of people and usually has a special affection with the older people.

MV - MV is the abbreviation for Music Video. MV is commonly seen on video platforms such as YouTube.

OTP - OTP is the abbreviation for One True Pairing. The phrase is common among fans and is used when talking about two members that they enjoy seeing interacting with each other with the most. It is also common among fanfiction and fan writings.

Netizen - Netizen derives from the words internet and citizen. A netizen is someone who has an online presence and is known for leaving comments on social media, news, forums, videos etc.

Noona - Noona is the female equivalent to Hyung. The term means older sister and is typically used by younger males.

Reality Show - A show that is designed to show the common people and fans a sneak peek into the daily lives of celebrities. The shows are typically streamed on Korean television but can be found on online video streaming sites such as YouTube and DramaFever.

Rookie - A Rookie is an artist or group that has only recently just debuted in the entertainment agency. Although there is no set time in which an artist can be considered a rookie, many fans think that artists that have debuted for less than one year are considered rookies.

Saesang - A Saesang is a fan that is overly obsessed with a celebrity to the point where they will do anything to meet their idols and to be remembered. This can be achieved by committing illegal acts or by physically or verbally abusing both idols and fans. Many Saesang fans have stated that they would rather be remembered for doing something negative, than not do anything and never be remembered. Being a Saesang is fan is looked down upon in the K-Pop community and they are commonly shamed among fandoms.

Selca - The Korean word for selfie (Taking a photo of yourself)

Sunbae - A senior that has been in the same industry as yourself for a longer period. They are typically older and have a higher-ranking status. It can also be someone that you look up to.

Teaser - A sneak peek or preview of new merchandise that has not been released yet. A teaser can be in several different formats such as videos, pictures, music etc.

7 Year Curse - The 7 Year Curse was a curse that was named by fans after several bands suffered great losses in the seventh year of their career. The curse is commonly linked to artists that are part of a group or band. The curse can be a great loss such as a member leaving a group or the group disbanding on the seventh year since their debut.

Trainee - A trainee is signed under an agency and is training to debut in the entertainment industry.

Trash - When you become obsessed with a certain artist and you find yourself collecting all their merchandise and albums.

About the Expert

Hayley Marland is a long time K-Pop fanatic with over 6 years of experience with dealing with the K-Pop community. Whether it is an attending concerts, buying merchandise or running group orders, she has experienced It all. Hayley spends her days watching K-pop, Korean dramas, writing reviews and actively participating on online forums related to Korean entertainment and music. Besides K-Pop, she enjoys getting creative by making different types of crafts, drawing, cooking and playing video games! She always likes to try something new and is up to the challenge.

HowExpert publishes quick 'how to' guides on all topics from A to Z by everyday experts. Visit HowExpert.com to learn more.

Recommended Resources

- HowExpert.com – Quick 'How To' Guides on All Topics by Everyday Experts.
- HowExpert.com/books – HowExpert Books
- HowExpert.com/products – HowExpert Products
- HowExpert.com/courses – HowExpert Courses
- HowExpert.com/clothing – HowExpert Clothing
- HowExpert.com/membership – Learn All Topics from A to Z by Real Experts.
- HowExpert.com/affiliates – HowExpert Affiliate Program
- HowExpert.com/jobs – HowExpert Jobs
- HowExpert.com/writers – Write About Your #1 Passion/Knowledge/Expertise.
- YouTube.com/HowExpert – Subscribe to HowExpert YouTube.
- Instagram.com/HowExpert – Follow HowExpert on Instagram.
- Facebook.com/HowExpert – Follow HowExpert on Facebook.